NIGHTMARES RUN LIKE MERCURY

By the same author:

Dancing Home (novel, 2016)
Story Ground: the Anthology (ed. with Jen Crawford, 2020)

NIGHTMARES RUN LIKE MERCURY

PAUL COLLIS

RECENT
WORK
PRESS

Nightmares run like mercury
Recent Work Press
Canberra, Australia

Copyright © Paul Collis, 2021

ISBN: 9780648936794 (paperback)

A catalogue record for this
book is available from the
National Library of Australia

Cover design: Recent Work Press
Set by Recent Work Press

recentworkpress.com

SS

For:

Bailey and Aria and Hamish and George,
my beautiful grandchildren.

And for:

Jai, Kaidon, Isaiah, Sariah, Zion, Nephi,
James, Violet, Ezra, Elka, Hope, Kenneth,
and beautiful Isaac.

I hope that beautiful words find you and fill
your spirit.

Contents

Through My Window

If you only see heat waves on an endless nothing,
and if you hate it, then close your eyes.
Don't poison yourself with the strain.
If you are sickened by the smell of saltbush on kangaroo,
block your nostrils; fill your nose instead
with your own familiar smells.
If its only sticky heat you feel upon your skin out there,
and you hate it...Wash yourself out.
Don't wear it.
You won't see what I know when I see through my window...
Nor will you smell the Country on every breath as sweet bush honey.
Brown snakes cover my home; black birds fill the sky...
I don't block out the sun when sweat is on my body— I keep it all.
Spring is the song on every Bee's buzz through my window,
—the smell of honey, drifting on wind from Black Wattle
in bloom is as beautiful as you...

2 Shades

Want a front row seat ride?

Wanna smell the sweat of fear?

—on skin?
Taste the sourness of race? ism?—
inside your mouth?
And;
hear fresh voice anguish?

'Then. Give me your tongue.
Step inside, then—Oh, you didn't know'?—('Like fuck, you didn't.')

Not consciously thinking—like an alley cat
Falling.
Tensions steps of black, and, of black-enough words.
Enough! Words.
More words, falling down, falling...
falling...
falling,
down like stars.

Behind the lines
stitched words, explain everything, away.
My dog, Will-Du, rolls his eyes.
Morphine sweats numb the life outa consciousness.
Swear words are the groundwork of deathness:-
'Black bastards'; 'Snowflake'; 'Coconut'.
Bottoms up,
side down.
Down, like falling stars.
Falling silence
with knowledge-attachment to Aboriginal bloodlines—
enlightened dreams dreamt enlightened dreamers

who imagine
denial—
who imagine
want?
who imagine
bravery?
while falling ...
falling ...
falling.
Down
like stars.

It Doesn't Look Half-Full to Me

No news from my cell-room.
There's no King in black slacks, here,
doin' no jail house rock.
Nothing to see, just some dust, a broom, and me.
I talk to Broom-Broom-
Broom-Broom always seem to have a handle on the situation.
I said, 'Hello Broom-Broom',
but, the broom isn't talkin' to me.

I tried sittin' like Buddha—up on my cell bed.
Tried, I did. But my legs don't like to bend like that.
Legs gave up the game in pain.

'Broom-Broom, what's a matter you? You got sore legs, too?
Huh? You give up on me too?
Come on. Don't I always take you out? Hey?
I told ya many times, we'll sweep the floor with the bastards.'

Day six—heading onto forever.
Captain's Log...

'Still no news from my cell-room
Broom-Broom still not talkin'—
I'm not talkin to Broom-Broom now, either.'

And if I were bank robber, with strong desire, for the cash,
I'd probably start drillin' my way away through the cell-room floor.
Fuck John-Paul and his 'freedom is getting to love
your prison cell' *shit-thang*.

I can't sleep no more. I may never sleep again,
but, then again,
I just might—
Depends...

If Broom-Broom can jest give me a sign...
I mean, I'm not askin for the impossible here,
not lookin' for the ultimate sign—
that one from the Big Gee in da sky...
C'mon Broom-Broom, lets sweep out the cobwebs.
See if I can get handle on the situation,
down here, on Desolation Road.

Shadow Walking

shadow walking—
Chapel Street.
Imagining what a New York woman does in the daylight.
Shiny people smell fresh,
but walk too fast.
They fly by, those determined slaves to the light.
Meanwhile...
　　　　　My wrecked head, aches.
Years of scatterings, of desires unmet, find me in new leathers.
All those people...
...But no shadow people in sight.
Every muscle tender, becomes a pain...
　　　　　　　　　...Every step, a nightmare in the light.

On The Spot

I came to this place, Your son.
Full of photos and young.
Unknown and unknowing myself,
Shyly learning new things.

The Thylacine was last seen in a Tasmanian zoo.

Scientist's say that it is extinct now.

The Thylacine is said to have been a shy creature who hunted the forests at night. With a head like a dog and a back with tiger stripes it was an apex predator. Found from Nui Guinea to Tasmania, it's nearest relatives were the Numbat and the Tasmanian Devil.

Both male and female Thylacines had a pouch. Four toes on the back feet, five on the front, it could stand erect like a wallaby. The jaws of the Thylacine were large, but the bite was weak—so weak that it could not kill a sheep. The Thylacine had high communication skills—a whining sound to identify itself across distance; a hiss (like a cat) when threatened, a yawn when scared; a guttural bark (like a dog) when hunting. The Thylacine had non-retractable claws. About the size of a medium size dog. A bounty was put on it by white people when they arrived in Australia, and in less than 100 hundred years, the Thylacine was wiped out by (white) people.

But I've heard story's that the shy Tiger has been seen in Barrington Tops in recent times—up around Gloucester. I hope, anyway.

My people believe that there's only 7 souls in the world and that a soul cannot reproduce nor die. We believe when a body dies, the soul goes immediately into the body of another living body...so, the shy Tiger is among us still, walking in night shadows so beautiful like the night.

Little Spirit Tiger

Little tiger, so beautiful like the night
With feet so thin and differing; Who are you now?
Have I met you on a cemented park? Under the stairs?
Little tiger, you who are designed to be night, so gentle, are you
Womboo? Ghost?
Do you run with Will-Du on-night skies,
and whine your name on wind, through the age?
Do you know me?

Games of Life

Circles of light pool away from stones in the green lake.
Hens glide past me.
And, further away, others run on water, towards crumbs.
They rush...
to be hand fed.
Colours red and blue; and black and white...and brown—
bill-shaped with spiked faces.
The birds of the feather, preen together
in the shallows, waiting for more...
They run the water top, again...to be hand fed by children,
who throw scraps into the green lake.
But, who else walked this water, before hand-fed fowls and Forts?
What black feet trod the stony bank? Who stood here?
What spear darted from beneath the shade?...Surprising attack
What light did shine black? Whose blood coloured the water?
Did the branch sigh?
Did the wind moan?

New footsteps make new tracks.
Clothes replace the naked.
Peewees and wood ducks fill a new scene.
Children run on full belly to play on the wooden fort.
And, waterfowl swim to me,
Having lost their fear of man.

Goin' Home

'How we git to Redfern?' he asked.
'I'll show ya, Brother.'

Hail a cab and off to the other world we sail.
Through city traffic we laugh, point at things.
They speak in language I don't know.
David does his best to interpret.
Whether he was telling me the truth, only they know.
He is happy. Can't wait to get there,
to be out of the light and into the black.
On the Block, a crowd comes a-runnin' to get a close look.
Beside the railway fence, next to other Brothers,
we made a place to drink.
The beer got drunk. We settled
into conversation, and the crowd thins away.
Green weed blows blue smoke, crooks and kickers drift 'round.
Cool dudes drive past in flash cars, looking us 'up and down'.
Others, less fortunate, hobble past in crooked style.
Some offer a sly smile as they hurry away to, the Lane—
where the gear is.
Cops drive past too, on another street.
Everybody breathes easier seeing the back end of their taillights
as they drive on to Newtown.
Sun-cast shadows hang over city buildings; the weather changes.
David and his Brothers speak to each other using body language—
shift the hip, bow the shoulder, blink an eye.
I know this language.
Wondering, 'What next?
Stay here and drink; or look for more yarndi?'
I leaned towards him and softly say, 'Brother. I gotta go.
Want anything? Or…You want me to take you back?'
Glassy-eyed, he looks into the fire.
'We right Brother. Thank you. Take care, hey?' he said,
as if talking to the flames.

Along 4 The Ride

Outside, out of uniform, unmarked—
he screams,
'Git out! Git outa the bloody car.'

Now, the shocked silence makes everything dead.
—carpark dead.
—words echo. . .
'Git out!'

Everywhere the words.

Pimpled youth looks scared—
He looks left.
He looks right.
Look out!

Rev the car, finger up, and back away.
Spun the wheels.
Away.
Free.

Blue upon red and blue, searching lights.
The kid scarped it.

Meanwhile:
In the mind of us mindless,
The boy's snarly, pimpled face mocked and haunted us, still.

Back to cloudy wine, and whiners,
inside the diner.

In protected walls we all paid
in plastic. Conversations and kids—
clean, pink, and safe.

Around the bend
was the end
for pimple-boy.
And in the final embrace,
the blue gum said grace.
And when the tow truck
cleaned the bark,
there was hardly a trace
of pimple boy.

Let Me Stay... So many points on the compass of love, there are...and, so many remain uncharted...

Let me stay,
till Forever smashes us.
I'll throw my heart to the ground,
to stay till then.
I'm crazy for your love, and in your lust dance with me...
then, dance on my heart. Stomp it to dust.
Don't shine a light—
I won't tell.
I won't share you around like other's have. You
will always be our secret.
You're the darkest star in any star-bright room.

Let me stay...
I'll smash Forever,
Let me love, we'll soak into each other's sweet sweat.
My blue lips here to kiss, to rip from my mouth for you.
And beneath the bloodied words, and in behind the folded green
—just be mine.
I'll wreck the wretches in me, just to see you.
Don't let closing time hold me away, Heaven.
I'll tear my shirt for you,
Let me stay.

Its not the body of a woman of which I speak

No, not that. What stole my attention

was more faithful, wilder, than any woman I'd met...

But I named her 'The Force'—speed was the drug.

This is my time in the dark...

I still worked, spasmodic, 'on the gas'.

So I didn't share Her around,

No other knew I was using

...So I kept it quiet, sweated and ached without her.

Wild times, I drove a slow car, crashed the wall, clipped a truck, bounced the gutter.

Sometimes, the night brighted like day,

Other times, everything turned blue.

Flashes of cotton in my bedroom never lasted long.

Some stayed too long, others were just dreams-slippers.

Oh, wild times in the dark—gassed-up and sweatin'.

More than a Pin-Prick

I'd become...
a public pain.
Did I make you, a little,
... sick?
Make me your vampire, then—
your time.
Take my neck.
Dig deep with kisses.
Let's feel the swirl of blood.
A country boy on Country is a power difference—making...
Spirit flying time with eagles—where everything's clear.
I'll never be clear.
Not in this life.
Not in any time.
But I can't keep my eyes from this changing sky.
Can't stop looking into your, blue...
Biaammi footprints out there show me the way...
You're there.
You're every watchtower.
You left your axe mark in Nyemba stone—On my heart.
You made the name and the sacred water...
Are they your tears, great Love?

Back in town:
It's rainy, cold and wet
so cold tonight...
Colder too, because I'm alone
away from you.
And it's a lover's night of holding close.
I love that being smuggled into each other's neck...
Yet, it doesn't feel like I'm in irons.

Eye's, Don't Blink

I remember you. You with the eyes.
I've seen before, that look—
I've seen those eyes— in sweet children— in Angel's
—and in devil's too.
Those eyes peer deep, burn inside. Never merely looking.
You, who have stood there, at the end of time,
have only one worthy question...
Why?

Ode to the Bong

My hungry hands steered the bendy
car. The highway road spoke volumes.
And boys looked back at us like stunned fish giggling.
My brother handed me the bong.
The bubbling bong sang along, breathing smoke—
like Puff The Magic Bong-A-Long.
'Here, have another' said my smoky Brother.
The more I had, the bendier I was.
And, the bendy car, smoked along too.

Spring

It's just too beautiful, this quite warm...
That play of light on water, that lone fisherman on the wharf.
Spring—Winter's gift to new life.
This beautiful day and opening act to brighter thoughts.
This young, new again feeling...
Those cut-off shorts.
And girls
With tattooed thighs that run like yesterdays.

And fish leap and gulls glide.
It's more than the yellow rays of sun
this Spring.

So pained, I've become,
at how my young people die, so young.
In life, I've stood at the funeral ground,
watching coffin's holding young Aboriginal people
being lowered away.
I've grieved an old man's grief, from my twelfth
birthday—
standing, watching my cousin being lowered.
And, I've grieved the passion of a Brother,
at the turning of the key
on my Brother(s)—
when they locked him away.
He went mad in there...
they released a man I didn't know.
He leaped into Forever, one sunny morning
from the Iron Bridge...
without making a sound.

Legends Die In Silence

You can never see how legend has been told to young fullas.
You could never see how we shake and were scared.
We young initiates whisper questions to Biammaii to quiet our shaking.
No longer under the protection of mother,
but on solid ground—our Mother Earth we stood,
in the shadow of history.
Law re-told by senior men strengthened our backs—
we boys stand together, solid.
...And we stand alone.
This is the way we become men.

Skinny legs tremble at the power of the story of our beginning.
But the tremble and worrying in us is broken
when we stand strong,
in law,
as men.

So far from our boyhood we stood silent, young men.
Silenced before our old men,
we look to meet their eyes.
And we take our place in history.
Knowing then, how we are important.

It was a quiet Sunday mornings, quiet as they mostly always are when the kids aren't there, I sat, people-watching. My car was unregistered, and I was broke.

I wrote this poem thinking about fall down broke, again, and, I thought, also, that about the only thing I seem be always left with are my words. I wondered if I could make it the city, where everything is in circles.

Writin' Cowboy(s) Unregistered Rodeos

Sunday sittin'. Quiet.
Unregistered.
10 dollar Bill, but, but, its eight seconds to make time.
Not vagrant, yet.
Ten bucks, left. But, but...
I've landed on my butt,
Only lasted six seconds...
In the dust, bent my eyes, west.
Home's somewhere there.

All those late nights and cheap weekends...I remember.
Sometimes, someone's on my mind. Wriggling around.
I fall down,
falling off the earth.
Back again, wriggling...
Wriggling, like Rainbow Serpent.

Here Isn't the News

What's that funny smell, Waku?
Womboo said Bilyara.
Ahh. Stink. Hmm.

What's that, over there, Bilyara?
Womboo said Waku.
Ahh. Ugly. Hmm.

What's that sound?
Black lightening?

Bang, bang...

> *Waku – the Crow, and Bilyara the Eagle discuss the sighting of the
> first white people to arrive on Barkindji country.
> No news of this was ever recited nor recorded as News of The Day in
> white peoples records.*

Barkindji feet did not have time to stand, nor run
the day the fires burned out.
A power burn smell and molten lead lingered a short while.
The fires died as the ashes colored red with Barkindji
near the birthing place.
Barkindji womboo spirits lost their homeland in the smoke
A new land for the taking – price: Free to the 'Settler'.

> *There is no record of the massacres at Toorale—another, no news day.*

B-B-Broken Spirit

Broken, was his voice...
b-b-broken he walked his country, that last time.
He didn't wear tattoos instead, initiation scars marked him
man-Barkindji.
Being wild-bred his culture kept him well fed.
He needed no white bred thing.
Cattle bells and hobble chains and scurvy ways
announced the end to his ancient ways.
Seven bells rang out: Christ On High! Christ Almighty! Christ is King!
Silence fell upon the man-Barkindji.
He danced up dust from Mother Earth, called Biammaii,
and covered, he lay down.
So don't ask me for whom that bell tolls, ask yourself such fool ways.
Turn and turnabout.
For from shadows new dawn will break,
and it will be you who are the zombies.

Colonised Place

Old Grandfather Hero said that we came from Wartu-Martie,
—we were the people from the 'big riverbank'.
The girls caught fish with their hands when the older sister's
gave birth beside Barka.
Babies were washed in Wartu-Martie and, announced as Barkindji.
In the cold months, we would not fish for the big Cod
because that was her birthing time.
Wartu-Martie wita witalana on all births
Wartu-Martie wita witalana on the returnings, also.
Full moons shone on Barkindji generations,
and then the town captured us
and held us in square rooms.
Barka cried for her babies voice, and then she dried...

and, then the Gubba's stripped her name
and now call her Wortumurtie.

Djingergulla Leaves No Trace

Years before years, when years has no number markings, Djinergulla's cut the tongue string of a person who broke the law.

Some say the Djinergulla carried a majik bag with dead men's bones things in it. They say that Djinergulla's always answered when Elders called him to 'do business'.

Djinergulla's left no mark upon a body or on the earth when he worked. He covered his feet in blood and feather shoes.

Some say Djinergulla's could fly and manifest themselves out of thin air.

Some say Djinergulla's covered their body in dead man's kidney fat—others say that he was covered in Emu fat...The string-cutter announced himself in death smell.

Djinergulla did not live with the people...He lived off to the side, on higher ground, alone.

No one knows how long he lived, but some say that only another Djinergulla can bury the feather-foot man.

No one knows who buried the last Djinergulla, but they found that there was a crystal placed at his head.

Hero Black, Remembered

Biammii changed shape at night.
One became two, Two Snakes—The Rainbow
One Snake, Guldabira, danced North.
The other, Wartanuring, danced South—down Menindee way.
Rainbow Snakes made the rivers. Made them join, in love.
Guldabira danced again, towards Wanaaring,
leaving water stones and ochre.
After the rivers joined the Rainbow Snakes became One again.
Biammii left the skins remnants on earth, and then
He returned to the sky.
Water stones bring water, ochre paint bring spirits into the body.
My River—Barka, she's empty now.
But I know where the water stones are...
I'll paint-up in ochre, and crush mica to add,
to make my black skin shine,
I'll dance and Biammii will see me.

Fly

Kick the door from the hinges
Fly.
Fly.
Wind will carry you this way.

Break the gate
Kick it to the ground.
Wind will carry you this way.

Smash the window, leave it in shards
Fly.
Fly.
Wind will carry you
to me.

Time Passenger

I sit and watch morning clouds burn.
The other side of town where questions drip,
ants rush, they rush.
They rush the train,
they rush the Doc.
Hide, look to hide,
look for a seat to ride.
Some come on late, some don't come.
Time passenger on a window seat
over there, where Cohen is—where the light is strong.
He said they can't hurt you there, so sing on...Sing on.

Now I See...

What relief, sleep,
no tremble in my spine...Now
no dry hot eyes singed, left to burn.

The powder burns on my lips
have melted into spit.

Oh, relief, with sleep that crept
on my broken.
You bastard.

No words, nor worlds can make it right again...
—no stoppin on the byways,
no breaks for coffee.

not like it had been.

Don't give me your Grace, God.
Don't show your face...to me.
Don't take my place...

Leave me,
leave me -
I'll do what I must
uptown, and down,
lookin' look...watch me.

leave me
my home is no more, no peace,
let it be.
Let it be.

Vapor Trails

Slowly the days pass.
Buses, cars, bikes
all roll away, away.
She is gone, down a shady street in shiny shoes.
Way above, vapor trails burn the sky
and way below, scars burn the land.
She screams, but I can't hear.
In another street, the new suits,
suit themselves, and colours burn red and gold.
Noisy bastards. Shut up! Open up! Give her   back.
A ghost slides up next to me. . .
I feel her now, can see her vapor trail—
These days, I keep my shoes clean,
Walking down shady streets.

Same Time/Next Year

And she puts it on
She puts it on in the morning
When she rises from the sheets.
And, Oh the golden sorrows now
I wait for tomorrow.
To bring her back to me.
Back to me.

Know well, oh grief. I see you.
How you deepen and take by surprise. Never leave.
And when she rises,
 it's painful and sweet. Her love, so deep.
It cuts through the flawed memory
—all at once, to think of those times, no matter how flawed.
I dream of her, rising.

I went to bed last night, feeling ashamed somehow of the softness and for 4 walls that held me safe—thinking about refugees and blackfullas living rough. I want to do something to help, but, I really only have broken words for blankets, ideas for food, hope for love...

So, today, I walked to my favourite coffee shop in Cook, feeling hungry, for today I will fast, and I'm hungry, and I have no money, and my hands are too sore to play guitar, so i won't be able to make coffee money, busking...But its okay, because I used to live on...

Lean Streets

sittin here, at Cook, watchin' people eat.
Thinkin' of lean days—of leanin' against lean streets.
...of sleepin' in cars, bent out of shape.
Puppy fat stripped, lined and sunken like yesterday.
Watchin' kids run past, at play.
mumma's milk warm their cheek,
while sittin' here, at Cook,
watchin' people eat.

I remembered the day I tried to speak up for myself. The Magistrate wouldn't hear my words. I was in Court for a traffic offence.

Trying to speak for myself was a mistake there, then. I was ordered out of Court and made take instructions for a Court appointed Public Solicitor. 'Just go along with what 'He' says, and you'll be over and done and out in a minute. Don't give 'Him' lip.' The Solicitor instructed me.

I did as I was told, copped a heavy fine and was dismissed feeling absolutely gutted. I turned at the door and looked at the Bench to see the magistrate staring at me, with eyes that seemed to be filled with anger toward me.

Similarly, years before this, at school, when I tried to tell stories of my people, of my Country, of us Barkindji people, and our spirituality, the teacher told me to 'Shut up!', He was teaching the class about his God and Jesus Christ. My beliefs didn't belong or fit nor 'dress his table of beautiful words.'

One Tongue:

Some things die,
Because you killed it.
Dismissed it and took it away,
You did. Deciding it don't belong,
That it don't fit with the proper things.
So you disabled it, and killed it,
Because it didn't dress your table of brilliant words.
You made your own things, live terribly alone, that day.

I asked my cousin when in Bourke a few weeks ago, how his younger brother was going.

'Yeah, he's going good, Cuz', was his reply.

Last night around 3am, I heard the death song of two birds outside in my garden. I knew the message the birds carry at that time in the night. I've been taught the culture from a young boy by my Elders. I knew a family member had died. As I lay on my bed, I wondered who it was that now had passed into the Dreaming. I thought of the dreams I'd been having over the past couple of weeks. His father's ghost- my uncle, had 'come to me' in my dreams, though I could not understand the dreams.

This morning, the phone call came announcing my younger cousin's sudden death overnight.

Away Without Words

From sleep into the Dreaming, you slipped
through in shadowed morning, silently.
No word of goodbye was offered as the then became the Great Forever.
In moonlit trees, the messenger's birds cried for you
as they sang your song.
I knew they were telling me 'someone is gone';
but I couldn't imagine, who.
Through my window, a shadow passed my bed with no form.
And, in the sun morning, in the stillness, came the message,
this time by telephone.
I know now that the passing was you.

I walked among the graves where faded images and the once remembered, but no longer visited, not by the look at the overgrown and fallen graves, in a world of the dead, in a Cemetery. Not even a bird, did I see there. The place was as dead as the dead.

Along the rows I walked, hands behind my back...looking, nodding to the names on the marble, on the wooden crosses... acknowledging the photos of the dead.

Once Remembered

2017, Sandgate Cemetery, revisited.

Date of Birth...Name...Date of Death
Always Remembered.

No one visits,
not anymore.
Grass grows where polished stone and wooden crosses stand,
weeds creep and strangle the forgotten names.
Photographed image fades to white. Everything white.
They were once remembered—once.

I was working at the meat works, in Newcastle, when Once In A Lifetime came out. Think I was 20 years old?

Amidst all that death and swear words...and those skunks, this most beautiful band tore through television screens and reached inside me, touching something in me that nothing else had been able.

Killers, at the meat works, laughed at him, 'singin' his silly faggot song—"Same as it ever was"', they scoffed!

'What do you think of the queer?' they asked me—the quiet one.

I quieted all of them with my words; 'Sounds great to me, man. They stand up for the downtrodden, the lost...for the environment. They ask 'why?' 'They're the best rock n roll band of this time...What's wrong with that?'

The killers hadn't spoken much to me before that. They didn't speak to me afterwards...I washed blood from the floor in the Beef House, my fingers blistered from the steam hose, I watched days go by...

and in honor of that song, and Talking Heads induction into the Rock n Roll Hall of Fame, I write...

Right. A Highway. . .

...find myself
...livin in a shot-gun, world...
    'How do I work this...'
Eventually,
questions run out on time,
      time runs out on life. . .
die a thousand times.
A thousand times.
A thousand ways.
Always,
same way.
Blade Runner, wanna take the ride?
            once a lifetime?
Blade stayed, stayed - cold in steel silence.
"How do I work this...?"
When moonlight rose as sunshine - where's Byron?
        where is that beautiful night?
      Life ran out on him...
and the dish-face wretches, ran away to spoon. Shadow skunks.
—hold nothing, in clean sheets...crawl
Hide. Hide and slide your pony ride,
skunks.
My God! *How do I...*

what have I done...?

The Cock Crowed Thrice, but Didn't Play Dice...

No
    one's awake...
                    not even *You*, God.
 The lightening's packed it in.
 Everybody's done.
             'Don't hang' she screams.
She slid...quiet down the window.
The frosted road drowned her voice in sticky tar.
Silent shadows hid that thief—Death.

Dirty Me, Bloody You

Life packed inside a pocket.
Bell:
Rise,
Wash,
Dress ....
Hit the yard:
anger into fear.
fear into fist.
Prison clothes hide hands,
inside dirty pockets.

Smashed a man . . .
He held my throat,
threw me out.
I pirouette,
threw a straight right—
A tendon snapped.
A bone broke.
Blood flew as sprinkles.

Different Rooms

Where
Am I
Here?
There, they are giggling at words like penises.

Opposite these rooms.

Yvonne's in dementia sleep, half dead.
Colour purples on her cheeks.
Every...
         Held...
                  Breath
Performed perfectly performed.
Eyes catch eyes.

Meanwhile, my poem stays rocked—stoned to death by words.
This poetry, my skin—
changes colour when I step into the light.
Sirens. Alarms.
Siren's smile, men stand alarmed.
Under arrest...
Into another room, the interview begins.
Again.
Black lines torn to bits in their breathy words.
My brother was handcuffed to a desk
Police bashed
every
Wor
d out
of
him.

Creative Deserts, Summer Storms

Living space and Santa Clause.
Childhood memories and grandfather's shores,
all leave me when I think of you, my child.
Your love is more than any wave, more than snow
and more than all, my love,
...all this you know.

Uncle Thomas

He asked if he could sing us a song.
His eyes, a blurry smoky purple.
That face that carried traditional story, smiled us a very old smile.
Yes, of course Uncle.
His voice carried the tune that last time;

he painted his island in the sun for us in song.

Un-named

he strode the bank of the Darling, a stranger.
And claimed it his. (Spit)
The stranger on the banks...
—that white Jesus, didn't even know her name. (Spit).
Grandfathers' seeing, black eyes would a told him—
'Barka. Thas her name. Barka—that one, there. Nhantarna. Nhantarna.
Barka. Barka.'
But the stranger didn't see the smoke of fires Barkindji.
Didn't smell gun powder that lingers on West wind,
icy and old, the memory of colour.

Instead, he strode the mountains, blind and parked Lawson.
Wrote white name upon Wiradjuri,
in that town—where streets are filled white.
There's ice wind of memory up there and river voices unheard.
We won't dance with the fiddle, rummed-up, nor dance with the Banjo.
Instead, cool fires and smoke, re-new our mother,
replace the smell of blood and gunpowder with small feet
dancing Wiradjuri dreams in colour.

My Nan was a keeper of our Law. She was solid and did never speak out of turn. She did not speak about the Law in gest, or threat. She held it safe to herself and for us. She was a good Law-woman.

When her time came to pass into the Forever, she didn't trust anyone to protect the Law as she had protected it, for her traditional culture had ceased being practiced. Rather than risk any corruption or violation of the Law at the time of her passing, my Nan took with her the secrets and the sacred back to the Dreaming.

Law woman

She came from dust
our law woman
desert heat and endless plain,
was made from smoke and rain.

She came from Dreaming
and held law.
Did business at night where dreaming is living.
Speaking with Spirit people

she moved spirit-shaped
kept dead-men things in her Majik bag, that no one
but her looked upon things sacred
secret.

Law-woman kept our Law safe.
Law-woman kept herself clean—no lie dressed her tongue.
When her waters broke, her child was washed in dust and made clean.
Law-woman was quiet, she didn't scream when he was born.
Law-woman was quiet when Police took her son.
She didn't call up war.
She didn't sing-up her Brother, Storm.
Her feet stayed still. She didn't dance-up her sister, Ghost-wind.
Instead, Law-woman sang her own death.
And Death came...
Law-woman's son arrived before she returned to Dreaming.
'Got somethin for me, Mum?'
Law-woman's eyes smiled her answer, in tear.
Her smile turned still.
Law-woman!
Law-woman!

Heart Thunderstorm

Barka's dyin...
no breath no breath
dust coughin through a dusty coffin, she's spread, dyin
purlu-kanirla pirnti-karntu
purlu-kanirla pirnti-karntu
wiimpatja— wathu punritj
watharna. wartharna.
gamoo. gamoo.
wartharna. wartharna.

Barka's dyin...
out of breath out of breath
dust coughin through (her) dusty coffin she's spread, dyin
heart attack...heart attack
my clan people
make it rain rain
give me water water
make it rain... rain.

What Has Men Done To You?

Oh, my darling,
River.
Barka.
Muddy water—
dry and drying,
where does Rainbow Serpent sleep tonight?

Who holds lover's dreams now?

Where are your guardians, Bunyip and Moona Gutta?
Can they rest without you?
Wide open, men left you, Barka.
Leaving you dirty dust.

How will the spirits of babies find their mother's now?

Through My Fingers

Its cold, rainy grey in the Can today.
So much the soggin' ground to sink.
Every step, a squelch into ancient soil.
Broken by wind and rain, the bones of my people speak.
And, in the North country, the land is fire dancing—
Burning life and limb.
Farther away, no eyes turned to see my love cough her last breath.
I rush, rush...
but too late.
Barka! Barka!
oh God, I can't recognise her.
Cold and spread dead, she lays.
I rush, rush...
For fun, two-strokes rip her dress,
without a sound they stripped her, hip to hip.
I have nothing to bury.
My arms fall right through,
leaving me grasping dust.
No tears of salt nor whispers,
or bright yellow flame of heat and prayer
will bring her back.
I reach inside me to hold her spirit, but fall sick.
I understand, that once given,
Death won't give up her dead.

Rebirth

'Blood filled eyes, lusted, then closed.

 Bloody streaks, the windows, a murmur dying...'

Washed myself in dark, warm water.

I couldn't see the bottom.

Out on the flat, warm wind wrapped around me,

and took me to a cradle of love.

With the brown kite,—my mother,

her nest—my bed, I'm safe from dogs,

I grew wings.

On hot thermals, I float.

Morning Blessing

Atop a Rock, our old Uncle led us,
and gently, he spoke to welcome the world...

An orange orb glowed beneath the earth's surface,
as an old, old wind flew to me.
My father came to me,
My grandmother came to me,
They wrapped me in the wind, held me tight.

It had been years since my father left us.
And it had been years since grandmother left
us. Their embrace held me as the first rays of light
reached me, bathing me in gold—
Their black son, bathed in gold atop a Rock, breathed in their presence.
 I heard the tapping from stone on stone
as the Elders marked the Rock in art.
Plaited hair from clans adored the patterns, and the wind held me tight.

The ages flew back and I was there, in that special place, beside the sea.
'Welcome, morning Sun,' Uncle spoke...
'Welcome to the East.
Welcome in the West.
Welcome in the North, and welcome in the South', old Uncle spoke.

Father and Grandmother were called back into the Great Forever,
Their leaving found me cold and marked by tears.
I wanted to cry aloud, 'Don't leave'
But everything has a place to be.

Thankyou East
And Thankyou West
And thankyou North
Thankyou South

And thankyou all.

Acknowledgements

Primarily, I thank and acknowledge Kunya, Barkindji, Wailwan, and Nyemba peoples for their continued commitment to the oral tradition of story.

I don't have my Mother's language—Kunya; nor do I have my Grandmother's language—Wailwan; nor do I have my Grandfather's language—Barkindji at my disposal to speak or express myself in.

This is because of the most savage attack upon my peoples by white people in their quest for our lands; and in their urgent control of my people in their process of colonisation.

And;

I want to thank and acknowledge the great friendship and support of Dr. Jennifer Crawford. Jennifer Crawford is not only a regarded and talented poet by colleagues and peers in her own right but is also, a dearest friend.

Cousin Sal, best gal pal;

Prof. Jen Webb, the best...

Ali Cobby Eckerman—best

Sam Wagan Dr. Watson, Black brother...

Dr. John Heath, always my brother...

Dr. Paul Magee, brilliant and kind man...

Dr. Jordan Williams, my friend, and teacher...

Byron for 'She Walks in Beauty'.

Dr. Julia Prendergast, border runner...

Aunty Kerry, beautiful soul, fighter, and poet (D).

KE, (the silent one), I thank you most of all for your kindness and friendship.

I do not have words enough to say how you all influence me. But, please know that you do.

And lastly, biggest thank you to a man who turned my head to poetry.

His words are stunningly brilliant.

Thank you to the one and only,
Lionel Fogerty.
Good on ya Brother Lionel.
Keep on Keepin on, man.

Thankyou to *Red Room Poetry, Cordite. Rabbit Poetry Journal* & *Australian Poetry* for publishing versions of some of these poems.

Many of these poems were produced as part of the Story Ground project supported by the Commonwealth Government Indigenous Languages and Arts Program, and the Centre for Creative and Cultural Research, University of Canberra.

About the Author

Paul Collis is a Barkindji person from Bourke, on the Darling River in north-west New South Wales. His novel *Dancing Home* was the winner of the 2016 David Unaipon Award, and was published in 2017 by the University of Queensland Press. He teaches creative writing at the University of Canberra, where he earned a PhD in Communications.

Printed in Australia
AUHW021139020522
363045AU00006B/8